My Look at the Chicago Bears Professional Football Club

JEROME WATKINS

My Look at the Chicago Bears
Professional Football Club

Copyright © 2021 Jerome Watkins

Revised Edition - February 2022

All Rights Reserved.

ISBN 978-1-7353091-9-4

Printed in the United States of America. No part of this book may be used or reproduced in any manner whatsoever without written permission except in the case of brief quotations embodied in critical articles or reviews.

Without limiting the rights under copyright reserved above, no part of this publication may be reproduced, stored in, or introduced into a retrieval system, or transmitted, in any form or by any means (electronic, mechanical, photo copying, recording or otherwise), without the prior written permission of both the copyright owner and the publisher of this book.

For information, contact:
Jerome Watkins
111 West Jackson Boulevard, Suite 1700
Chicago, Illinois 60604

My Look at the Chicago Bears Professional Football Club—1st Edition

Cover and Interior Layout & Design:
Tarsha L. Campbell

Published by:
DOMINIONHOUSE
Publishing & Design, LLC
P.O. Box 681938 | Orlando, Florida 32868
407.703.4800 phone
www.mydominionhouse.com

Dedications

*To my father, Daniel Watkins,
and my sons, VaShon and Torres.
Each one of you is my hero and inspiration.*

Contents

Introduction

Chapter 1
My First Visit to Historic Soldier Field 9

Chapter 2
The First Time I Was Personally Introduced To Chicago Bears' Football Player 15

Chapter 3
Sunday Afternoon, December 12, 1965 21

Chapter 4
How I Became Interested In Becoming A Football Referee 25

Chapter 5
I Started to Referee High School Football Games in 1974 29

Chapter 6
Preparation on Game Day 35

Chapter 7
Chicago Bears Coaches & Players & My High School Teachers 41

Contents

Chapter 8
The First Time I Worked on a Football
Chain Crew............................ 47

Chapter 9
My 2006 Football Season 51

Chapter 10
The National Football Conference (NFC)
Championship Game..................... 57

Chapter 11
August 11, 2016
One Memorable Evening 65

Chapter 12
An Incredible Moment,
One Shining Moment 73

Chapter 13
One Hundred Year Celebrations 79

Chapter 14
Overtime 89

Chapter 15
Torres First Regular Season NFL Game...... 93

Endnotes............................. 100

• • • • •

"...This started me on a journey, unbeknownst to me as a kid, so that years later, I am able to share this exciting and joyous expression of: My Look at the Chicago Bears Professional Football Club."

INTRODUCTION

At the age of eight, in 1959, I was playing football with the neighborhood kids at Tuley Park in Chicago, Illinois, at 90th Street and South Park Way (the street name was changed to King Drive after the assassination of Dr. Martin Luther King Jr. in 1968).[1] At that age, I had no idea—or even a dream—that I would work on the sidelines of a Chicago Bears professional football game at historic Soldier Field in Chicago for the National Football League (NFL). This started me on a journey, unbeknownst to me as a kid, so that years later, I am able to share this exciting and joyous expression of:

My Look at the

Chicago Bears

Professional Football Club

"I first heard the phrase 'Monsters of the Midway' as a kid, and now, as a member of the Chicago Bears football chain crew, I have proudly stood next to the various coaches on the Bears sideline who wear their Monsters of the Midway sweatshirts on some of the colder weather game days."

Chapter 1

My First Visit to Historic Soldier Field

I remember that my first visit as a fan to historic Soldier Field for a professional football game was on August 6, 1965, for what was then known as the College All-Star game, which was played by former college star football players who had been drafted by the different NFL teams. The College All-Stars played against the NFL team that had won the NFL Championship game the season before, which, in this case, was the Cleveland Browns. The *Chicago Tribune* newspaper, in 1934, had sponsored the first College All-Star game between the NFL champions and college stars. The All-Star game was an annual summer tradition here in Chicago until 1976.

I remember Jim Brown of the Cleveland Browns playing, and rookie Dick Butkus, who had played in the All-Star game. Dick Butkus had played football at Chicago Vocational High School and at the University of Illinois and was drafted in the first round as the third overall selection of the NFL draft

*My Look at the Chicago Bears
Professional Football Club*

by the Chicago Bears in 1964. The 1965 draft was actually held on November 28, 1964.

Like most young boys between the ages of eight and ten, my attention was drawn to football in general and in particular to watching the Chicago Bears professional football team. As a kid, I tossed around a football and played with other neighborhood boys at Tuley Park. I have a vivid memory even today of playing with other kids in the park, and it was fun.

I remember when Gale Sayers was drafted in the first round by the Chicago Bears. He was the fourth overall selection for the 1965 NFL draft out of the University of Kansas. As a star running back at the University of Kansas, Gale Sayers was known as the "Kansas Comet."

I watched the Chicago Bears on television when the team played at Wrigley Field, and the owner and coach of the Chicago Bears was Mr. George Stanley Halas. Mr. Halas was also one of the founding fathers of the NFL, in addition to being a player.

My interest in football probably peaked in 1965 when Gale Sayers, who was also known as the "Galloping Ghost," scored six touchdowns in a game in his rookie year against the San Francisco 49ers on Sunday, December 12, 1965.
In 1965, the NFL was a fourteen-team league, and the cities with an NFL franchise were the following:

- Baltimore Colts
- Chicago Bears

*My First Visit to
Historic Soldier Field*

- Cleveland Browns
- Dallas Cowboys
- Detroit Lions
- Green Bay Packers
- Los Angeles Rams
- Minnesota Vikings
- New York Giants
- Philadelphia Eagles
- Pittsburgh Steelers
- San Francisco 49ers
- St. Louis Cardinals
- Washington Redskins

The Chicago Bears' first season at Soldier Field was in 1971, after spending fifty seasons at Wrigley Field (1921–1971), the home field of the Chicago Cubs Major League baseball team.[2] This connotes a special link between football and baseball in Chicago, between the professional sports teams, the Bears and the Cubs, playing their respective games at Wrigley Field, where millions of fans have attended to see their team play. Soldier Field is an American football stadium located on the south side of Chicago, on the lakefront, which is situated next to the shore of Lake Michigan, one of the five Great Lakes. Soldier Field opened in 1924 and is now the home field of the Chicago Bears NFL professional football team.

The Chicago Bears moved from Wrigley Field to Soldier Field for the start of the 1971 football season, and their first game at Soldier Field was September 19, 1971. The Bears

My Look at the Chicago Bears Professional Football Club

defeated the Pittsburgh Steelers 17 to 15 before a capacity crowd of 55,701. Soldier Field is one of the oldest areas in the NFL. It was built in twenty months and reportedly holds the shortest construction time for a modern-day stadium on record. The stadium serves as a memorial to American soldiers who have died in wars. It was designed and planned in 1919 as a memorial to the soldiers of World War I. Soldier Field opened on October 9, 1924, as Municipal Grant Park Stadium, changing its name to Soldier Field on November 11, 1925.

I first walked onto Soldier Field on Sunday, November 11, 2001, as a member of the officiating chain crew that worked the Chicago Bears home games. The Bears' opponent that day was the Green Bay Packers. I was privileged to work on that field seventy-six years after the date of the name change from Municipal Grant Park Stadium to Soldier Field. It was an honor to be in such a significant place as I began an up-close-and-personal look at the Chicago Bears, on what is celebrated as Veterans Day in the United States. On that Veterans Day, my look at the Chicago Bears involved the Bears playing one of the oldest and most popular teams in the NFL, the Green Bay Packers.

The Bears became known as the "Monsters of the Midway" by dominating the sport with four NFL titles in the 1940s, starting with a 73 to 0 championship victory over the Washington Redskins in 1940, which gave rise to their nickname. It has been said repeatedly that the Bears—or as some would say, "Da Bears"—is the city's most beloved sports team here in Chicago, and there is a richness to their

My First Visit to
Historic Soldier Field

hundred-year history. I first heard the phrase "Monsters of the Midway" as a kid, and now, as a member of the Chicago Bears football chain crew, I have proudly stood next to the various coaches on the Bears sideline who wear their Monsters of the Midway sweatshirts on some of the colder weather game days.

"Not only was Mr. Howard an educator, he had been among the first of the African Americans to reintegrate to play in the NFL in the 1940s, with the New York Yanks and the Cleveland Browns. Mr. Howard played in the NFL from 1949 to 1953 in the positions of half back on offense and defensive back on defense. Mr. Howard was the second person I personally met who played professional football in the NFL."

Chapter 2

The First Time I Was Personally Introduced to a Chicago Bear

The first time I was personally introduced to a Chicago Bears football player was in either 1959 or 1960. My childhood home was in the 600 block of East 89th Place, and Mr. Willie Herman Lee, who was a member of the Chicago Bears, lived with his family on the 600 block of East 90th Street, which was around the corner from my home. Mr. Lee was drafted by the Chicago Bears in 1954, in the twenty-third round. Mr. Lee played the position of offensive tackle and offensive guard. He played with the Bears in the NFL for nine seasons (1958–1966). He wore number 70, and I remember even today seeing Mr. Lee proudly wearing his Chicago Bears football jacket.

Mr. Lee was a member of the 1963 NFL Champion Chicago Bears. The 1963 Championship was the Bears seventh NFL Championship. The Bears franchise's first league title had been a 10 to 7 victory on December 4, 1921, under what was called the American Professional Football Association (APFA), which was later renamed the National Football League (the NFL). The Championship game in 1921 started the Bears toward a total of eight franchise championships, and Mr. Lee helped play an important part in championship number eight overall for the Bears by being part of the 1963 NFL Championship. The Bears' 1963 season record was 11 wins, 1 loss, and 2 ties.

In September 1965, on my first day at Harlan High School, Mr. Sherman John Howard was my first teacher (physical education) for my very first school period of the day. At Harlan High School, Mr. Howard was the football coach and athletic director, as well as a physical education teacher. Not only was Mr. Howard an educator, he had been among the first of the African Americans to reintegrate to play in the NFL in the 1940s, with the New York Yanks and the Cleveland Browns. Mr. Howard played in the NFL from 1949 to 1953 in the positions of half back on offense and defensive back on defense. Mr. Howard was the second person I personally met who played professional football in the NFL. Starting with the 2019 football season, the NFL celebrated a hundred years as a professional football league, and Mr. Howard had helped the NFL reach that magnificent milestone.

In September 1969, I started as a freshman at Elmhurst College, where Mr. Calvin Saunders was my college roommate and classmate for the school year. Calvin would later become the brother-in-law of Mr. Howard. Calvin was instrumental in and directly responsible for having me start a career as a basketball referee during our college days. I did not play football for Coach Howard at Harlan, and I did not play on the college football team at Elmhurst College, even

*The First Time I Was Personally
Introduced to a Chicago Bear*

though my college roommate Calvin was an outstanding college athlete and captain of the college basketball team. Nevertheless, I was able to follow my very first high school teacher, Mr. Howard, to the NFL, and I accepted that as a very high honor.

Mr. Howard (Coach Howard) had a great influence on all of his students over the years at Harlan High School where as coach he encouraged each of us to do awesome work in our respective careers and endeavors. I was in the presence of greatness at Harlan High School for four academic school years. Mr. Howard was my teacher, motivator, and role model. He was called Coach throughout his teaching years and continued to be called Coach after he retired from the Chicago Public Schools. As I mentioned, I first met Mr. Howard in September of 1965, and I was blessed, as were so many students, to walk the halls of Harlan High School for four years (1966–1969) and have him as one of my teachers.
 Another teacher of mine at Harlan was Ms. Melissa Tatman, my English teacher. Ms. Tatman planted a seed in my life, and in each of her students, just as Coach Howard did. Ms. Tatman made an indelible impact on her students and helped to shape countless lives, and you can witness the same indelible impact on her nephew, Chicago Bears running back Coach Charles London. Coach London and I greet each other when I work a Bears home game at Soldier Field, and we wish each other a good game.

Coach Howard and Ms. Tatman nurtured their students with skill and patience. Quite frankly, they were my two favorite

My Look at the Chicago Bears
Professional Football Club

teachers at Harlan. I remember Coach Howard actually getting in the school swimming pool during swimming class to demonstrate a technique that he was teaching. Coach Howard showed by example. He was just an outstanding educator. When I entered Harlan High School as a freshman in 1965, little did I know then that I was being prepared by my very first high school teacher, Mr. Howard, to follow him to the NFL, not as a football player, but as a member of an officiating chain crew, standing on the sidelines next to the players and coaches in the biggest sports organization in the world. The interest and dedication that Coach Howard and Ms. Tatman exhibited to each of their students was just simply outstanding, and I was fortunate to have Coach Howard as my teacher at Harlan High School.

Now that I look back and reflect over my growth to this day, I can appreciate that Mr. Howard took on the responsibility to plant a seed in my life, setting a strong foundation for all of his students to carry on, study well, work hard, keep good values and integrity in our life, and always—and I mean always—take the moral high ground in life. Coach Howard's and Ms. Tatman's former students are eternally grateful.

● ● ● ● ●

"In ordinary everyday life, I did run into or, alternatively, crossed paths here in Chicago with Herman Lee in 1959 or 1960, who lived around the corner from my childhood home on East 89th Place."

Chapter 3

Sunday Afternoon, December 12, 1965

On Sunday afternoon, December 12, 1965, Gale Sayers tied the NFL record of six touchdowns in a 61 to 20 victory over the San Francisco 49ers in the mud at Chicago Wrigley Field. I did not see the game but read about Gale Sayers's feat the next day on my way to elementary school.

Gale Sayers scored, in order, on runs of 21 yards, 7 yards, 50 yards and 1 yard. He scored on an 80-yard pass from Rudy Bukich and on an 85-yard punt return while playing on a muddy field at Wrigley Field. In his rookie season as a Chicago Bear, Gale Sayers scored a total of twenty-two touchdowns in 1965, which is an NFL rookie record.

I did not have a chance to see Walter Payton play in person, though I did see him (number 34) play when I watched the Bears on television. As a Bears fan, too, I was ecstatic when Walter set an NFL rushing record on October 7, 1984, at Chicago's Soldier Field, surpassing Jim Brown's career rushing record of 12,312 yards. On that game day, versus the

My Look at the Chicago Bears Professional Football Club

New Orleans Saints, Walter was the new NFL leader, with 12,400 yards. It was also Walter's fifty-ninth career 100-yard game, also breaking Jim Brown's NFL record. Walter played thirteen seasons with the Bears (1975–1987), and finished his career with 16,726 total rushing yards and a total of 110 rushing touchdowns.

I heard and listened to the "Super Bowl Shuffle," and I enjoyed the music, which was a rap video brashly taped by twenty-four members of the Bears on November 23, 1985, when the Bears had a 11–0 record to that date and were Super Bowl favorites. The rap video broke into the Billboard's Top 100 at Number 92 the week of January 11, 1986. With Walter Payton, Jim McMahon, William Perry, Otis Wilson, and Willie Gault among ten singers and musicians of the twenty-four teammates participating, it became a nationally recognized phenomenon and peaked at Number 41 during the week of February 8 to 15, 1986, a week after the Bears had won Super Bowl XX (20).

In ordinary everyday life, I did run into or, alternatively, crossed paths here in Chicago with Herman Lee in 1959 or 1960, who lived around the corner from my childhood home on East 89th Place.

I remember greeting quarterback Bobby Douglass in a financial institution in downtown Chicago in 1973 on a weekday afternoon. Bobby Douglas was the Bears quarterback from 1969 to 1975. As a quarterback, Bobby Douglass was one of the Bears' most effective rushers,

*Sunday Afternoon,
December 12, 1965*

averaging 6.6 yards a carry for a total of 2,470 yards, and he scored twenty touchdowns. It was exciting watching Mr. Douglass play football; he played hard and displayed excellent energy as a quarterback.

I met quarterback Vince Evans in person and spoke with him in a clothing business in downtown Chicago. Vince Evans played for the Bears from 1977 to 1983, seven football seasons.

I did not know at the time when I met Herman Lee, Bobby Douglass, and Vince Evans in person that years later, I would grace the sidelines in the NFL and have a personal and up-close look at the Chicago Bears as a member of the officiating chain crew working the Bears home football games—the same Bears sideline that Gale Sayers, Walter Payton, and so many Bears players graced with their presence.

● ● ● ●

"I returned to my college dormitory room the next night, and I found in my desk an envelope with three dollars in it. I asked my college roommate, Calvin Saunders, where the money had come from, and he said that I'd got paid for being a referee."

Chapter 4

How I Became Interested in Becoming a Football Referee

I first became interested in becoming a football referee in the fall of 1973 while I was watching an NFL game on Monday Night Football. It looked fun and interesting watching the football referees on the field working the game. I could not tell you, for the life of me, what two teams were playing on that fall Monday night, but that game appealed to my interest in becoming a football referee.

I had registered with the Illinois High School Association (IHSA) during the summer of 1973 to become a licensed basketball official. I had graduated from Elmhurst College that past May, and while in college, I had started to referee basketball games for the college intramural program on campus.

It is interesting how I got started. I walked into the college gym one night, and a person was needed to referee one of the scheduled college intramural basketball games, and I volunteered—or so I thought. That was in January, 1972. I did not know at the time that I was being paid to referee that basketball game between my college peers. I returned to my college dormitory room the next night, and I found in my desk an envelope with three dollars in it. I asked my college roommate, Calvin Saunders, where the money had come from, and he said that I'd got paid for being a referee. Calvin was in charge of assigning students on campus to referee the intramural basketball games. He was also the captain of the college basketball team, playing the position of center, and he was a starter for his entire four-year college career at Elmhurst College. I told Calvin to sign me up to referee more intramural basketball games on campus.

Mind you, in 1972, on a college campus, to referee a college intramural basketball game for three dollars a game was some valuable expense money. Also, during my junior year in college, I worked in the college cafeteria after lunch and dinner every day cleaning dishes, drinking glasses, and silverware. During my senior year in college, the 1972–1973 academic school year, I was the student manager of the cafeteria staff that cleaned the dishes, drinking glasses, and silverware. I was paid twenty-five cents more an hour as the student manager, due to my additional duties and responsibilities. The base rate was two dollars for each student employee cleaning dishes. The money I was making from my job in the campus kitchen increased my monthly expense money.

During my senior year in college, I was a resident advisor (RA) in Schick Hall, which was the only co-educational college dormitory on campus. Each RA in the various

How I Became Interested
in Becoming a Football Referee

dormitories on campus was paid for this position. I was also a referee once again in the Elmhurst College intramural basketball program on campus during my senior year. In that senior year in college, my college activities and my employment opportunities had me receiving finances from three separate sources. In addition to my activities and employment on campus, I made the Dean's Academic List in my last semester as a college student.

I was also introduced to being a referee by my maternal uncle Marion Price. At the age of either ten or eleven, I would go with my uncle to basketball games every Saturday during the basketball season to watch him referee. My uncle Marion took me to his basketball games for several years. Now that I look back and reflect on that experience, my uncle was planting a seed in the life of his nephew, and for that, I am forever grateful. Today, I make certain that I inform my uncle Marion each time I work with the football officiating chain crew at the home football games of the Chicago Bears. I continue to referee basketball games today, in the year 2020.

• • • • •

"In the summer of 1979, I attended the West Coast Football Officials Clinic in Southern California. The word "clinic" is used to symbolize a classroom setting for teaching and learning. I was one of the approximately ninety-five football referees from across the United States who were in attendance to learn and improve our knowledge, skills, and techniques to become better football referees."

CHAPTER 5

I Started to Referee High School Football Games in 1974

I started to referee high school football games in 1974. I have also refereed college football games, and when I was asked to be a member of the Chicago Bears chain crew, also known as the line-to-gain crew, in the year 2001, I was bringing to the NFL twenty-seven years of experience as a referee officiating at football games.

As much as I may admire the home team that I was hired by, as a referee, I cannot cheer and be a fan. I must remain professional in my duties and responsibilities before, during, and even after the game has ended. I sign a Code of Conduct Agreement with the Chicago Bears (which, in part, is also on behalf of the NFL) at the beginning of each new football season, which I pledge to adhere to. Although I am looking at the Chicago Bears, I cannot and should never display fan-like enthusiasm and excitement while working a game. My conduct and the way I carry myself have to be most professional at all times. No matter how well-intended fans may cheer and celebrate the joy and excitement the game may bring to them, a member of the chain crew is not allowed to visibly cheer and celebrate the outstanding plays and team victories.

In the summer of 1979, I attended the West Coast Football Officials Clinic in Southern California. The word "clinic" is used to symbolize a classroom setting for teaching and learning. I was one of the approximately ninety-five football referees from across the United States who were in attendance to learn and improve our knowledge, skills, and techniques to become better football referees. That football clinic was where I was introduced to Dr. Laird Hayes, who was the director and organizer of the clinic. My attendance at the clinic was a good learning experience. At the conclusion of the three-day weekend, during the final class session, Laird acknowledged each attendee by name and had a positive, upbeat, and supportive comment regarding each one of us. What is remarkable to me is that Laird learned something about each of the ninety-five attendees within a three-day weekend.

Laird Hayes went on to officiate for thirteen years as an on-the-field football referee in the Pacific Coast Conference, the college conference also known as the Pac-10 Conference. After several successful seasons as a football referee in the Pac-10 Conference, Laird Hayes then became a football referee in the NFL, starting the 1994 football season. Laird became one of the premier on-the-field football referees during a distinguished career in the NFL. He retired at the conclusion of the 2017 season, after having an outstanding

*I Started to Referee High School
Football Games in 1974*

twenty-three-year career as an NFL referee, working the position of side judge. During his NFL officiating career, Laird worked three Super Bowls: XXXVI (36) in 2002, XXXVIII (38) in 2004, and XLVI (46) in 2012.

I had the good fortune and opportunity to work the Green Bay Packers versus Chicago Bears game on November 11, 2001, that Laird Hayes had been assigned to work as one of the on-the-field football referees as a side judge. In the NFL in 2001, the on-the-field officials were the referee, umpire, head linesman, line judge, field judge, side judge, and back judge. To work this game while Laird was working was just an incredible experience, and it was fun for me. I started to reflect on when I had first met Laird in 1979 in Southern California, and there we were on that day, November 11, 2001, and I was working in the NFL with Laird Hayes.

Ten years later, on Sunday, January 23, 2011, while I was working the National Football Conference (NFC) Championship game between the Green Bay Packers and Chicago Bears in Chicago, Laird was approximately 460 miles away in Pittsburgh, Pennsylvania, working the American Football Conference (AFC) Championship game between the New York Jets and the Pittsburgh Steelers. That presented a special feeling in my life and continued an amazing connection with my friend Laird.

The winners of the AFC and NFC games would play in Super Bowl XLV (45) two weeks later, on February 6, 2011, in Arlington, Texas. The Green Bay Packers won that Super Bowl, beating the Pittsburgh Steelers.

Congratulations, Green Bay!

In the NFL, when the first half has ended, when the chain crew and teams return to the field after halftime to start the second half, the chain crew members switch sides to work the game on the other team's side of the field. I worked on the Green Bay sideline for the first half of the game. My look at the Chicago Bears was from directly across the field from the team. In the first half, I was standing on the sideline of the Green Bay Packers, working that professional football game. That created such excitement and enthusiasm for me, to be there working in historic Soldier Field, especially on Veterans Day, Sunday, November 11, 2001.

• • • • •

"In working the different positions, I was being enriched by having an entirely different perspective of each game that was being granted to me on game day by my unique sideline vantage point. The sideline vantage position allows you to see the professional NFL football game and hear the sounds of the players on the field."

CHAPTER 6

Preparation on Game Day

The preparation on game day in the NFL begins before the chain crew goes onto the field to work the football game. The members of the chain crew are required to arrive at the stadium and be present in the locker room two hours before game time. The chain crew has a pre-game meeting with the linesman who is assigned to work the game by the NFL. In the pre-game meeting, the linesman covers details for that game with each crew member, going over their particular duties and responsibilities and emphasizing the importance of working collectively to make certain that the game goes smoothly for each team.

During this pre-game meeting, the linesman discusses movement on the sideline for the chain crew members and the importance of moving when the players are running to your sideline. In other words, he discusses making sure that the chain crew members get out of the way. The two chain crew members working the yardage chains for the 10-yard measurements are instructed to take the yardage chains and physically move away from the sideline and allow the

My Look at the Chicago Bears Professional Football Club

players to continue and complete that play, as they may go out of bounds on that sideline. Also, movement on the sideline keeps the chain crew members from being injured or knocked down. In the past, chain crew members, on occasion, have been run into, and a few have been actually knocked down. We are a part of the contest being played, and there is physical contact with the chain crew members at times. The linesman would discuss our personal safety in detail.

I started as an alternate chain crew member in 2001, thereby affording me the opportunity to work different positions on the chain crew on game day. I have worked the position of front-chain stick, rear-chain stick, penalty report card, line-to-gain indicator, clip man for the yardage chain, down and distance recording, and the drive-start marker. Each position requires a specific detail, and the position that you are assigned for that NFL game is crucial. Whatever position I am assigned to work on game day, I strive to be truly professional in every way. As a member of the officiating chain crew and being afforded the opportunity to work a different position each game, I always want to do a proper job as a "sideline referee."

In working the different positions, I was being enriched by having an entirely different perspective of each game that was being granted to me on game day by my unique sideline vantage point. The sideline vantage position allows you to see the professional NFL football game and hear the sounds of the players on the field. You also have a firsthand view of

Preparation on Game Day

the speed that the players bring to that NFL game. To watch an NFL game on television is one thing, but having an up-close view gives you a much different perspective.

Your movement on the sideline from time to time causes you to bump into players and coaches on the sideline, and, on a rare occasion, I remember running into and pushing a player out of my way so that I would not be injured or hurt. At the same moment, I had to keep in mind that those NFL football players were significantly stronger than me. The physical strength and size of the players is amazing, and I am privileged to stand by their side while working an NFL football game. This NFL game is being seen by thousands of fans who are in the stadium and also seen by millions on television. Any given NFL telecast, and, in particular, a Super Bowl game, is seen by millions of viewers around the globe. A Super Bowl game has been seen by an estimated 140 million viewers worldwide.

The chain crew work to keep an accurate accounting of each down and distance for a new first down or touchdown, and this information or data is consistently recorded and kept on the sideline by a chain crew member for each play of the game. This particular aspect of the game is so crucial, and the chain crew has the responsibility of making certain that it goes smoothly for each team while that team has possession of the ball or, alternatively, while the opponent is playing good defense and has not allowed their opponent to get a new first down or touchdown.

My Look at the Chicago Bears Professional Football Club

The smooth conduct of the game, in part, is dependent upon how well the football referees on the field work with the timekeeper and, more importantly, with the members of the chain crew. The football players are actually playing the game, but the members of the chain crew are important because we keep the game moving smoothly. We are assistant officials who are part of the officiating team for each NFL football game. We add to the smooth administration because we are an integral and important part of the game. Each NFL team assigns its own men and women chain crew members to work all of that team's home games, which include the pre-season, regular season, and playoff games; however, you actually work for the NFL.

In working with the chain crew, my look at the Chicago Bears has allowed me to work pre-season games and through the regularly scheduled NFL season, which has included several Chicago Bears playoff games. I worked the NFC Championship game between the Green Bay Packers and Chicago Bears on Sunday, January 23, 2011. This was a fun game to work. I also had the opportunity to work the Chicago Bears and Philadelphia Eagles NFC Championship game on Sunday, January 6, 2019.

There are several perks to being a member of the Chicago Bears chain crew. Each member receives a parking pass to each game, including the playoffs—provided the Bears make the playoffs that football season. We are fed at each football game, provided with food, plenty of water, and soft drinks. We are paid a stipend for each game that we work. To be a part of an NFL officiating chain crew is a big thrill.

● ● ● ● ●

"On game day at Soldier Field, various players engage with me in conversation on the sideline before, during, and after the game. The first Bears player to initiate a conversation was R. W. McQuarters, who wore number 21. R. W. just started talking to me during my first regular season game on November 11, 2001, and he carried on a good conversation on the sideline."

Chapter 7

The Chicago Bears Coaches and Players and My High School Teachers

The head coach for the Chicago Bears for my first game on November 11, 2001, whom I stood next to on the sidelines at Soldier Field was Dick Jauron, and during his tenure, the Chicago Bears had thirty-five outstanding team victories. The next head coach I stood next to was Lovie Smith, who started his coaching debut with the Chicago Bears at the start of the 2004 season. Coach Smith guided the Bears to Super Bowl XLI (41) on February 4, 2007, during his outstanding tenure as the Bears head coach. Coach Smith compiled eighty-four victories as head coach, advancing to the playoffs three times during his nine-year tenure, advancing to two NFC Championship games and a Super Bowl.

Marc Trestman was the Chicago Bears coach during the 2013 and 2014 seasons. Coach Trestman lead the Bears to thirteen victories. During John Fox's tenure from 2015 to 2017, the Chicago Bears were led to fourteen victories. Coach Matt

My Look at the Chicago Bears Professional Football Club

Nagy, who started with the 2018 NFL football season, is the fifteenth head coach of the Chicago Bears in their franchise history.

Mr. Arthur Blank, the owner of the Atlanta Falcons football and the Atlanta United soccer teams, greeted me when I was working the Bears–Falcons game on Sunday, September 10, 2017, when I was on the Falcons sideline during the second half of the game. Mr. Blank stood next to me for a brief moment and spoke to me. It is a custom in the NFL for a team owner to visit his team's sideline for the final minute or so left in the game, particularly to greet people. I found Mr. Blank to be very personable.

On game day at Soldier Field, various players engage with me in conversation on the sideline before, during, and after the game. The first Bears player to initiate a conversation was R. W. McQuarters, who wore number 21. R. W. just started talking to me during my first regular season game on November 11, 2001, and he carried on a good conversation on the sideline. R. W. was a member of the Chicago Bears from 2000 to 2004, for five football seasons. Defensive cornerback Brock Vereen, who wore number 45, was another player I directly spoke to at each home game. Brock and I would always talk before the opening kick-off and wish each other success and a good game. Brock was a member of the Chicago Bears for the 2014 and 2015 football seasons.

Brock's brother, Shane Vereen, played with the New England Patriots from 2011 to 2014 as a running back. Shane played with the Patriots when they won Super Bowl XLIX (49). Interestingly, on January 26, 2016, Brock signed a futures

*The Chicago Bears Coaches and Players
and My High School Teachers*

contract with the New England Patriots. The two brothers, who had grown up in Valencia, California, played in the NFL at the same time.

Charles London, the running backs coach, and I would greet each other before each Bears game, starting with the 2019 season, the Chicago Bears' Centennial season. Coach London returned to Chicago and was hired by the Bears on January 12, 2018, and this was his first season as running backs coach, though he had previously (2007–2009) served as an offensive assistant with the Bears. Coach London had nine previous seasons in the NFL. He became known to me personally during the summer of 2019, even though I had stood on the Bears sideline next to him during his continued tenure with the Bears for the football seasons of 2007, 2008, 2009, 2018, and 2019, the Bears' Centennial season.

As mentioned above, Coach London's aunt Melissa Tatman had been my high school English teacher at Harlan High School. Our graduation class of 1969 celebrated its fiftieth class reunion over the weekend of July 27 and 28, 2019, with a dinner dance and Sunday picnic. Ms. Tatman informed me at the all-class Harlan High School picnic that her nephew Charles was a coach for the Chicago Bears. I mentioned to Coach London eleven days later (on August 8) at the Chicago Bears–Carolina Panthers pre-season game that his aunt Ms. Tatman had been my high school English teacher. This created a special connection between Coach London and me, and each of us made certain that we greeted each other at the start of each Bears home game during the Centennial season.

My Look at the Chicago Bears
Professional Football Club

Ms. Tatman championed each one of her students at Harlan to strive above and beyond their learning capabilities in the same fashion as Coach Howard, my physical education teacher, and I was privileged to be a student in Ms. Tatman's English class and Coach Howard's gym class.

During my first year as a member of the Chicago Bears chain crew in 2001, standing next to coach Dick Jauron, the NFL consisted of the following thirty-two franchises:[3]

- Arizona Cardinals
- Atlanta Falcons
- Baltimore Ravens
- Buffalo Bills
- Carolina Panthers
- Chicago Bears
- Cincinnati Bengals
- Cleveland Browns
- Dallas Cowboys
- Denver Broncos
- Detroit Lions
- Green Bay Packers
- Houston Texans
- Indianapolis Colts
- Jacksonville Jaguars
- Kansas City Chiefs
- Miami Dolphins
- Minnesota Vikings
- New England Patriots
- New Orleans Saints
- New York Giants

*The Chicago Bears Coaches and Players
and My High School Teachers*

- New York Jets
- Oakland Raiders
- Philadelphia Eagles
- Pittsburgh Steelers
- San Diego Charges
- San Francisco 49ers
- Seattle Seahawks
- St. Louis Rams
- Tampa Bay Buccaneers
- Tennessee Titans
- Washington Redskins

● ● ● ● ●

"It's an honor to have had the opportunity to work every NFL game that I have been privileged to work. I started my preparation for my officiating experience as a kid on a Sunday afternoon at Tuley Park in Chicago."

Chapter 8

The First Time I Worked on a Football Chain Crew

The first time that I worked on a football chain crew, holding the marker-yardage sticks so that a football team would know how far their team had to advance the football down the field for a new first down, was when I was ten or eleven years of age. This happened during a grade school football game at Tuley Park, at 90th Street and King Drive in Chicago. At the tender age of ten or eleven, I had no idea or anticipation that approximately forty years later, in the year 2001, I, Jerome Watkins, would be working the football chains as a member of the Chicago Bears chain crew, working the Bears home games in the NFL. I was asked to work on the Chicago Bears chain crew by Wayne Endicott, whom I first met in 1973 when I joined the Athletic Officials Association (AOA), which is a training association for basketball and football officials.

When you as a football fan attend a professional football game in person or watch a game on television, you will see that the chain crews in the NFL wear distinctive vests so that we are easily recognizable standing on the sideline

*My Look at the Chicago Bears
Professional Football Club*

of the football field. In the NFL, our vests have black and yellow vertical stripes. The official uniform for the chain crew today consists of black pants, with a 1-inch white stripe on the side of the pants from the waist to the cuff, and a black leather belt, 1¼ to 2 inches wide, with a plain buckle. The required socks are black. Each chain crew member is issued football officials athletic shoes, a white knit short-sleeved shirt with the NFL logo, and a blue baseball cap, and for the colder weather, a blue knit cap. Each member of the chain crew is also issued a blue pullover for rain, a blue jacket for cold weather, and blue jogging pants. The chain crew's appearance on the sideline always looks good, and the professional manner in which each of us works during the football game makes the game go smoothly.

My first year as a member of the chain crew (starting with the 2001 NFL football season) was as an alternate. As chance and good fortune would have it, for my first season, I worked the game between the Packers and Bears on Sunday, November 11, 2001, where the attendance at Soldier Field was 65,630 and the playing time of the game was 2 hours, 59 minutes. Final score: Packers 20, Bears 12.

It's an honor to have had the opportunity to work every NFL game that I have been privileged to work. I started my preparation for my officiating experience as a kid on a Sunday afternoon at Tuley Park in Chicago. Whether it's a grade school game at Tuley Park or an NFL game at Soldier Field, each member of the chain crew is there to work that game to give the players a good and enriching game

The First Time I Worked on a Football Chain Crew

experience. When you are working the game, it is very difficult to explain what it actually feels like when you are on the sideline and see the players' excitement and hear the fans' enthusiasm. It is a great feeling. It is a feeling "unlike any other."[4]

As always, my father, Daniel Watkins, was very happy for me when I shared with him that I would be working as a member of the official chain crew for the Chicago Bears home football games in the NFL. I wanted my father to also share my joyous and happy expression on that Sunday afternoon, November 11, 2001. There has always been a special bond between my father and me. My father always believed in me, and he was always very encouraging. My father has always been my inspiration and always inspired me to do good and live a rightful life.

As a father myself, I strive to always inspire my sons, VaShon and Torres, and I make a great effort to create a special bond between my sons and me. As a fraction of our fatherhood, so many fathers, including me, utilize sports, in part, as a springboard to a college education, or a career, or an entrepreneurship, or as a sole proprietor and a chance to explore the wonders and riches of this wider world.

⊢ • • • • • ⊢

"The 2006 football season was a good season for me. I worked three Chicago Bears games as an alternate with the chain crew. Also, my team of high school football referees and I worked the first and second rounds of the Illinois High School Association (IHSA) football playoffs."

CHAPTER 9

My 2006 Football Season

On Sunday, January 23, 2011, Bryan Bulaga, a rookie that football season and a starter on offense for the Green Bay Packers, was playing his first NFC Championship game in his first year in the NFL, and I was working the football clips for that championship game. It was the first championship game for each of us.

I first met Bryan Bulaga on August 26, 2006, while Bryan was playing on his high school football team at Marian Central Catholic in Woodstock, Illinois. I was working the game on the field with the high school football referees: Mike Reier, the lead referee; Ed Reier, the line judge (and Mike's brother); Mark Chesharek, the umpire; and Gary Swanson, the linesman. I worked the position of back judge. My son Torres worked that game as one of the ball boys.

That night, as the captains were being escorted to the center of the field for the ceremonial coin toss to start the game, I remember asking Bryan whether he thought he would be playing in the NFL one day. I asked Bryan this question, in

My Look at the Chicago Bears
Professional Football Club

part, because of his large physical size at that time as a high school senior. His response, in a very humble manner, which I believe was very sincere for a high school senior, was, "I am not sure." As my high school football referees worked that game, I noticed that Bryan was a very good football player. Actually, he was an outstanding player; he plays the game of football very well.

The 2006 football season was a good season for me. I worked three Chicago Bears games as an alternate with the chain crew. Also, my team of high school football referees and I worked the first and second rounds of the Illinois High School Association (IHSA) football playoffs. In the first round of the playoffs, a total of 640 referees were selected to work, and 256 high school teams qualified to participate. In the second round, a total of 320 referees were selected.

The high school football playoffs in Illinois is exciting in itself. For each playoff game that I have been assigned to work, electricity just fills the air, and you can literally feel the enthusiasm in the stadium, especially just before the opening kickoff. You can feel the emotion that is present.

As luck and good fortune would have it, Mike, Ed, Mark, Gary, and I were selected and assigned to work the second-round game on November 4, 2006, between Lemont High School and Marian Central Catholic in Woodstock, Illinois. My son Torres accompanied the football crew that night; he was working as a ball boy at Marian Central Catholic for the second time that football season. What a privilege and an honor for Torres at nine years old. I worked the back judge position, and Torres went with me to the clock operator's booth before the game so that we could discuss the operation of the game clock with the clock operator and provide him and the game announcer with the football referees game card, which had the names of each referee and the football positions we were working in the playoff game that night. Unbeknownst to either Torres or me, we had no idea that years later, Torres would have an opportunity to visit the game clock operator at Soldier Field in Chicago and learn how the game clock is operated during a professional football game in the NFL.

As on-the-field football referees, we are required to work each game with integrity, use good judgment, and work the game in accordance to the rules and football mechanics so that we may administer the rules consistently and fairly. It is an honor to work a high school football game where you are able to enrich the lives of high school students. That Saturday night, November 4, 2006, we found ourselves working a game involving Bryan Bulaga and his Marian Central Catholic team for the second time that season. Marian Central Catholic had a successful victory in their first-round playoff game, which allowed them to advance to the second round, and the overall ratings of the football referees that I was working with allowed us to be selected for this second-round (IHSA) playoff game.

When Torres and I would arrive at the respective high schools I was assigned to referee, I would ask the head coach of one of the teams that was playing if Torres could work with their ball boys (and some teams had girls as ball persons as well) for the game. Torres was welcome to work as a ball boy, and at some games, with luck and to his benefit, he worked as the only ball boy for that high school sophomore or varsity team. His football experience and knowledge of the game of football started at five years of age.

I have worked some high school games as a referee in the position of back judge. In Illinois, under the IHSA, one of the pre-game duties when you work the position of back judge is that you visit the school's stadium booth where the game clock timer and official game announcer work. Torres was by my side as he accompanied me to the booth where I provided a game card, with all five football referees' names for the public address announcer and an 8-by-11-inch laminated chart of the official football signals, which also included the penalty enforcement for the 5-, 10-, and 15- yard penalties for the announcer to use for reference during that football game.

Since I was going to start that NFC Championship game on Sunday, January 23, 2011, working on the Green Bay Packers sideline, I introduced myself again to Bryan Bulaga, who was the starting offensive tackle (number 75) for the Packers that football season and for that championship game. I asked Bryan if he remembered me when I worked his high school games at Marian Central Catholic in Woodstock. Bryan answered that he indeed remembered me. That was a proud moment—being remembered—and even prouder because I

My 2006 Football Season

was working my first NFC Championship game in the NFL. The Bears–Packers game on January 23, 2011, was hyped as the biggest football game in Chicago history. The winner of that game would win a ticket to Dallas for Super Bowl XLV (45).

"Working on the chain crew is a small part of a professional football game, but it is a very exciting and very important part. The chain crew makes it possible for the game to go smoothly for each team. The work that you are doing is very important, and you are close to the action of the game."

Chapter 10

The National Football Conference Championship Game

I worked the NFC Championship game between the Green Bay Packers and the Chicago Bears on Sunday, January 23, 2011, at Soldier Field, which sits on the lakefront of Lake Michigan, and it was a cold afternoon. Nevertheless, it was an exciting day, a day full of great anticipation, especially for a victory by the home team. That entire day just had you feeling good inside, whether you were a fan of either the Packers or the Bears, a player on the Packers or Bears roster, one of the referees on the football field, or a member of the chain crew, like me. It was an honor to be working on the sideline as a member of the chain crew for that NFC Championship game.

The members of the chain crew were instructed to arrive early, two hours before game time (4:00 p.m., Chicago time). I arrived at Soldier Field about two and a half hours before game time. I was one of the three alternates on the chain crew working that game. There I was, preparing to work that rivalry between the Bears and Packers, which is the heart of the NFL and its oldest rivalry, and on that day, I was a part of

My Look at the Chicago Bears
Professional Football Club

that historic sports rivalry in the most lucrative sports league in the world. The winner of that NFC Championship game would play in Super Bowl XLV (45), two weeks later.

Soldier Field was packed for the game. The attendance was 62,377, millions were watching it on television, and I was fortunate enough to be participating. There was excitement and a high level of professionalism for those of us working that game. The chain crew took a group picture before the singing of the national anthem. Military jets flew over Soldier Field as the national anthem was reaching the final crescendo. This was a thrill in itself, and you could literally feel the emotion in that place.

I was working what is called the clips, which means that I would place a football official's clip on the actual chain that helps to determine if the team with possession of the ball is able to advance down the field for a new first down. I had to be accurate when placing the clip on the yardage chain, which intersected either the 5-, 10-, 15-, 20-, 25-, 30-, 35-, 40-, 45- or 50-yard line as a team advanced the ball down the field for a possible first down. My placing of the clip was an absolute mark during first-down measurements.

1 was also responsible for marking down each penalty on a penalty card for that championship game. There are seven items that must be recorded on a penalty card: 1) what quarter of the game the penalty was called in, 2) the time in the quarter the penalty was called, 3) the team the penalty was called on, 4) whether the team was on offense or defense, 5) whether the penalty was accepted or declined, 6) the number

*The National Football
Conference Championship Game*

of the player on whom the penalty was called, and 7) the referee on the field who made the call.

At halftime, I provided the penalty card to the linesman, George Hayward, for his review and any corrections that needed to be made. The card was given back to me for the third and fourth quarters. When the game ended, I gave the penalty card back to the linesman, who would subsequently turn it in with the information to the NFL office in New York City so that it would accompany the game films, which are diligently perused by the NFL to help evaluate the on-field referees' performance. My work that day required a high level of concentration and attention.

Working on the chain crew is a small part of a professional football game, but it is a very exciting and very important part. The chain crew makes it possible for the game to go smoothly for each team. The work that you are doing is very important, and you are close to the action of the game. You are able to see while working on the sidelines how fast and agile the players are. The players' athleticism is simply remarkable, and it is exciting to see this athleticism up close. In high school and college football games in this country, people who work the chains will almost always work on one sideline for the entire game. In the NFL, you work on one sideline during the first half of the game, and then you switch to the other side of the football field after halftime. As an example, for that championship game, I started the game working on the Green Bay sideline. When I came back on the field after halftime, I worked on the Chicago Bears sideline. The chain crews switch sides each NFL game, whether it's

My Look at the Chicago Bears Professional Football Club

pre-season, regular season, or the playoffs, including that NFC Championship game. This is the standard practice throughout the NFL for every football game.

In addition to me, the chain-crew members working that championship game were Harold Schwind, our crew chief; Tony Alvizu; Neal Pringle; Joe Slayton; Mark Endicott; and Tom Hall. During the regular NFL season, Mark Endicott, Tom Hall, and I work the Chicago Bears home games when an alternate is needed. On this Sunday afternoon, the three of us had the opportunity to work that championship game.

I was working the clips and penalty card. Harold Schwind worked the down box, for the first, second, third, and fourth downs, and he recorded each down and distance that the team with the ball had to advance for a possible new fifteenth down. Tony Alvizu was working the front-chain yardage-marker stick. Tom Hall was working the rear-chain yardage-marker stick.

Harold Schwind, Tony Alvizu, Tom Hall, and I started the game working on the Green Bay Packers sideline. Joe Slayton was working the unofficial down box for the first, second, third, and fourth downs. Neal Pringle worked the drive-stick marker, which is placed on the yard line when a team has possession of the ball to start their advancement down the field. The drive-stick marker stays on the yard line until the team with possession of the ball scores a touchdown or kicks a field goal or the other team gets possession of the ball. Mark Endicott was working the unofficial line-to-gain marker and mat, which shows the team with the ball the line that team has to reach for a new first down. This position

The National Football
Conference Championship Game

required Mark to mirror the forward-chain person (Tony), who was directly across from Mark on the other side of the field.

That day, Joe Slayton, Neal Pringle, and Mark Endicott started the game working on the Chicago Bears sideline. When halftime was over, Harold Schwind, Tony Alvizu, Tom Hall, and I worked on the Chicago Bears sideline, while Joe Slayton, Neal Pringle, and Mark Endicott worked the game from the Green Bay Packers sideline. Your responsibilities remain the same; you just switch to the other team's sideline for the second half of the game.

The linesman for that NFC Championship game, George Hayward, congratulated each member of the chain crew for working the game, which he said was an honor. The on-field football referees included the referee, who wears a white-colored baseball cap, linesman, umpire, line judge, field judge, side judge, and back judge.

The Packers scored first in the first quarter: score 7 to 0. The Packers scored in the second quarter: score 14 to 0. Neither team was able to score in the third quarter. In the fourth quarter, the Bears scored a touchdown: Packers 14, Bears 7. With 6:04 left in the fourth quarter, the Packers scored again: Packers 21, Bears 7. The Bears scored on a four-play drive, with 4:43 left in the game.

Final score:
Green Bay Packers 21
Chicago Bears 14

*My Look at the Chicago Bears
Professional Football Club*

I worked that NFC Championship game, and it was a fun game to work. Two weeks later, the Green Bay Packers won Super Bowl XLV (45), beating the Pittsburgh Steelers.

Congratulations,
Green Bay Packers!

• • • • •

"To look across the field there at historic Soldier Field and see Torres working a professional football game was just great. For me, it was exciting to have father and son working a professional football game together as part of the football officiating chain crew."

Chapter 11

August 11, 2016:
One Memorable Evening

My look at the Chicago Bears professional football team reached a high point on August 11, 2016, when I looked across the football field and saw my son Torres working that professional football game between the Denver Broncos and the Chicago Bears. Torres, a good-looking eighteen-year-old who would be starting his college classes as a freshman eleven days hence, was working the drive-stick marker. An eighteen-year-old, entering college student was working a professional football game with his father. That night had another special touch: Torres and I, for the past three summers, had visited Denver, Colorado, and during the last two summers, that had coincided with the particular weekend of my birthday. Torres and I had traveled to Denver, Colorado, six different times since 2006 for several different reasons: 1) I had scheduled teaching assignments and had the opportunity to teach and lecture, 2) we attended either a football or basketball sporting event, or 3) we were celebrating my birthday on August 8.

My Look at the Chicago Bears Professional Football Club

Torres and I arrived at Soldier Field approximately two and a half hours before game time and proceeded to the officials' locker room. There was the regular pre-game meeting with the linesman, during which we covered the duties and responsibilities of each of the chain crew members. At the conclusion of the meeting, I assisted Torres with the NFL-issued football pants, which are adjustable, the white NFL knit shirt, the black-and-yellow vest and the blue, NFL-issued baseball cap. Torres wore black shoes with black socks. He looked very good and professional. He had a good, youthful presence about him that evening.

We walked from the officials' locker room onto the field, and when we reached the field, Torres's exact comment was, "This is so cool!" So, that night of August 11, 2016, was a proud moment in my life. As a father, that was one memorable evening. I was working with my son in that professional football game in the NFL. Talk about a happy father—that was me!

The respective chain crew members walked the field, which means that in twos or threes, you walk around the field between the sidelines and the structure of the stands where the fans sit. Before each Chicago Bears home game, fans are allowed to stand on the sidelines, on the outside of the actual playing field, and be close to the players as the players stretch, run, and throw the football to prepare for the start of the game. Torres and I walked around the entire field together, and I was able to introduce my son to the various other game-day persons working that game, such as the groundskeepers and ball boys.

August 11, 2016:
One Memorable Evening

For that Thursday-evening pre-season game, my position to work was the rear-chain-stick marker for the first down, and across the football field was my son Torres, working the drive-stick-marker position. The drive stick marks the start of every new ball possession for the team on offense. Torres would stay at that mark until there was a score by the team in possession of the ball or there was a change of possession, meaning, when the other team got the ball.

What also made that evening so memorable was that after halftime, Torres worked a second position for the chain crew, taking what is called the unofficial line-to-gain position. The unofficial line-to-gain is when you have the marker (pole), which you are holding by hand, and you are also responsible for the orange-colored carpet or mat that is placed on the ground outside of the sideline to the playing field so that the team with the football will know that they have to reach that carpet, that that particular yard line will get their team a new first down.

Joe Hall was not feeling well at halftime that evening, so the chain crew made adjustments so that Joe could continue working. Joe worked the drive-stick position, and Torres worked the unofficial line-to-gain position. Torres had the opportunity to work two separate positions during his very first pre-season football game with the Chicago Bears chain crew in the NFL.

It just happened that Torres was on the Chicago Bears sideline the first half, working the drive-stick marker, and for the second half of the game, Torres was on the Denver Broncos sideline, working the unofficial line-to-gain position. That position required Torres to mark the line to gain for the first down. He mirrored the forward-chain person on the other side of the field. Torres was looking across the field at the Chicago Bears sideline during the second half of that NFL game.

To look across the field there at historic Soldier Field and see Torres working a professional football game was just great. For me, it was exciting to have father and son working a professional football game together as part of the football officiating chain crew. My son Torres was being afforded the same sideline vantage point for that NFL pre-season game that I experience each NFL game that I have an opportunity to work on the sidelines here in the NFL. I was blessed with a good look at the Chicago Bears, and across Soldier Field, I could see my son looking at the Chicago Bears play the Denver Broncos.

When Torres accompanied me to my high school football games that I was assigned to work as a referee on the football field for the IHSA, he, along with other ball boys, made certain that the referees were given the correct team ball when that team would start their possession of downs. In the NFL, the ball boys are an important part of the smooth flow of the game. Likewise, in high school, the ball boys are also important and help with the smooth flow of the game. On occasion, if the high school football game was being televised, you would see Torres on television. Torres

August 11, 2016:
One Memorable Evening

started accompanying me to my high school games in the fall of 2002 at the age of five years old, and, over the years, Torres could be seen running the football to the field, to the referees, and, in particular, to the umpire.

On the evening of August 11, 2016, Torres could be seen on the Fox Television Network working with the Chicago Bears chain crew in the NFL, all while having a close-up look at the Chicago Bears and Denver Broncos. Before kick-off, as Torres and I walked the field together, Torres commented, "These players are huge!" Torres himself is slim in stature and stands about six feet tall or so. With his physique, he looks like a basketball player. Torres did play on his junior high school basketball team at Hill Junior High School in Naperville, Illinois, and on the freshman basketball team at Metea High School in Aurora, Illinois.

Torres radiated his joy that evening, which was just another beautiful moment for me to see in his life. What makes the night of August 11, 2016, so special is that Torres and I had visited Denver from August 6 to 8 . We had no idea, had not even imagined, that upon our return back to Chicago, Torres would have the opportunity to work a pre-season professional football game with his father in the NFL. Torres had football knowledge and awareness as to how to work with a football chain crew even at the professional football game on August 11, 2016, between the Denver Broncos and the Chicago Bears, now that he was eighteen years old. It was easy for Torres to fit right in with the Chicago Bears chain crew, or, as some would say, "fall right into place."

My Look at the Chicago Bears
Professional Football Club

Incidentally, for the second straight year, the Chicago Bears played their first pre-season game against the Denver Broncos at Soldier Field on August 10, 2017. Torres's look at the Chicago Bears that evening involved him visiting the clock operator's booth before the game, where he learned firsthand how the NFL game clock is operated. After that learning experience, Torres watched the pre-season game from the stands, about seven rows behind the Chicago Bears team bench near the 30-yard line.

In visiting the clock operator's booth and thereafter watching the game as a fan, Torres continued his intimate look at the Chicago Bears football team and the NFL on that beautiful, warm summer night.

"As I continued to referee high school football, my sons, VaShon and Torres, shared incredible and amazing experiences with me on Friday nights and Saturday afternoons at my high school football games."

CHAPTER 12

An Incredible Moment, One Shining Moment

My next scheduled game to work in 2016 with the Chicago Bears chain crew was for Monday Night Football, September 19, 2016, the home opener for the Chicago Bears versus the Philadelphia Eagles. Joe Hall, who had been a member of the chain crew for twenty-five plus years, said to me that night that it must have been a very good feeling to have my son Torres working with me for the pre-season game on August 11. I responded with great excitement and happiness that yes, it was a good feeling.

Joe Hall's son Tom is a member of the Chicago Bears chain crew, and Joe has experienced the joy and happy feeling of working at Soldier Field with his son, who is also registered as a football referee with the IHSA.

On August 11, 2016, I had the opportunity to work and share an incredibly big moment with Torres, my son, and, in return, Torres had a great opportunity to work and share an

My Look at the Chicago Bears Professional Football Club

incredibly big moment with his dad. That was a good look at the Chicago Bears by a father and son together at Soldier Field on that warm and beautiful summer evening.

As I continued to referee high school football, my sons, VaShon and Torres, shared incredible and amazing experiences with me on Friday nights and Saturday afternoons at my high school football games. I am reminded of a quote that President George Herbert Walker Bush, the forty-first President of the United States of America, our Chief Executive, so eloquently stated during his presidency (1989–1993): "There is nothing better in America on a Friday night than a high school football game." My sons, VaShon and Torres, have been by my side while I have had the great opportunity to referee on Friday nights at high school football games here in America. Those Friday nights have been some of the greatest times I have shared with each of my sons: "The best day is a day I spend with you."

So, in answering Joe's question to me after some reflection, and though I answered yes, that it was a good feeling having Torres work with me for the Chicago Bears–Denver Broncos pre-season football game, it continues to be a good feeling for me.

Torres, my son, my hero and inspiration, shared that pre-season game with me, with all of the excitement and all of the joy and satisfaction of working an NFL game. Torres experienced all of the fun that I've been privileged to enjoy by being a member of an NFL chain crew. This was one shining moment for me, a phrase I have adopted from "One Shining Moment," the musical selection associated with the

*An Incredible Moment,
One Shining Moment*

National Collegiate Athletic Association (NCAA) March Madness Basketball Tournament.[5]

My son VaShon started accompanying me to my high school football games when he was eight years old and continued each consecutive year thereafter until he finished junior high school and entered high school in the year 2000. He worked as a ball boy at my high school football games, which caused his transition to high school for his academic studies to go very smoothly. It was a great feeling for me. VaShon learned fast and was very dependable as a ball boy. He interacted and engaged with other ball boys and the high school football coaches.

VaShon's active participation helped to make the games I refereed go smoothly and created a good flow to the game by making certain the football referees had the footballs ready and in place for each team. VaShon visited the game booths with me before each of my games when I worked the back judge position to provide the game cards that introduced the five referees for the public address announcer and game clock operator.

What I was putting in place with VaShon were experiences that I would also share with Torres. I experienced many "shining moments" every Friday night during the high school football season with VaShon by my side. VaShon was leading the way for my later shining moments with Torres on Friday nights. VaShon, Torres, and I created meaningful father-and-son time together with our Friday football nights

My Look at the Chicago Bears
Professional Football Club

when we visited different high school communities. I had no idea, and it was truly way beyond the grasp of my own imagination, that when Torres started accompanying me to my high school football games at five years of age, he would one day stand on the sideline of a Chicago Bears football game at historic Soldier Field.

The first high school football game to which Torres accompanied me was Bolingbrook High School in Bolingbrook, Illinois, in 2002. Calvin Saunders, my college roommate, was the varsity boys basketball coach at Bolingbrook High School, and I had the distinct pleasure of introducing Calvin to my son.

VaShon and Torres have created many shining moments in my life that have been absolutely perfect, and for that, I am eternally grateful.

An Incredible Moment,
One Shining Moment

VaShon

Torres and Bobby

• • • • •

"I attended the Bears 100 Celebration Weekend (June 7–9, 2019) as a fan. It was indeed a once-in-a-lifetime event for everyone in attendance. The entire weekend was an outstanding celebration full of exuberance and excitement."

Chapter 13

100 Years Celebration

On May 20, 2017, I was fortunate to participate in the 100 Years banquet celebration of the Athletic Officials Association (AOA) where I started my officiating endeavor in basketball and football. It was my forty-fourth year as a member when the association celebrated this hundred-year milestone.

The AOA is the oldest officials association in Illinois and, arguably, the oldest officials association in the United States. The AOA is a training association and provides quality officials for sport contests. I joined the AOA Basketball Division in the fall of 1973 and the Football Division in the fall of 1974. Each year, the AOA selects inductees to the AOA Hall of Fame based on nominations by the Football Division. Consideration for nomination is given to individuals who have been AOA members for at least ten years and have contributed positively to the AOA, to the officiating community, and to high school sports.

My Look at the Chicago Bears Professional Football Club

On November 7, 2017, I was inducted into the AOA Football Division Hall of Fame at the annual banquet and awards presentation at the end of the high school football season. I was presented with a beautiful plaque engraved with my name, Jerome Watkins. I wrote the following letter after the banquet and awards presentation, and a copy was mailed individually to Ed Stanley, Bob Foster, Joe Hall, and Harold Schwind.

November 7, 2017

Just a note to let each of you know that since I joined the Athletic Officials Association of America 44 years ago, in 1973, that I have followed in your footsteps.

I have worked High School football games over the years with each of you, and also Wayne Endicott. I have also travelled to the State of Indiana with Ken Trainor to watch him and his football crews work football games.

I have been fortunate since the year 2001 football season to work with each of you at Chicago Bears football games at Soldier Field as a member of the chain crew and also at the University of Illinois when the Bears played while Soldier Field was being remodeled for the 2002 NFL season.

I have continued to follow in your footsteps by working the Illinois High School Association football finals in 2008, working a 2008 Championship Game, the SA final.

100 Years Celebration

On this evening of November 7, 2017, I was inducted into the AOA Hall of Fame, so I join you there.

What an honor for me to be inducted the year of the 100 year anniversary of the Athletic Officials Association of America (AOA), 1917 to 2017.

This great milestone was celebrated on May 20, 2017, with an anniversary banquet. The AOA continues to pursue excellence in training referees and the AOA is continuing the 100 year legacy.

I am reminded of the famous poem titled "Footprints in the Sand," and in particular the last line which reads...

...it was then that you carried me.

I attended the Bears 100 Celebration Weekend (June 7–9, 2019) as a fan. It was indeed a once-in-a-lifetime event for everyone in attendance. The entire weekend was an outstanding celebration full of exuberance and excitement. That celebration weekend was in advance of the upcoming NFL 100th football season in 2019. The Chicago Bears are the only franchise in the NFL that celebrated its centennial at the same time as the NFL, with the 2019 football season. The celebration weekend featured appearances by more than one hundred Bears alumni, seven Hall of Famers, Head Coach Matt Nagy, and the 2019 Chicago Bears team. That Bears 100 Celebration was the largest collection of former and current Bears ever assembled. The 100th football season

My Look at the Chicago Bears Professional Football Club

of the Chicago Bears in 2019, was my sixtieth year of looking at that team since my youth in Chicago, and it was my nineteenth year as a member of the Chicago Bears chain crew working the Bears home football games at historic Soldier Field. The Chicago Bears football team started their 100th football season with an NFL leading of 778 victories.

On February 13, 2020, I was in Kansas City, Missouri, at the Negro Leagues Baseball Museum (NLBM) at 18th and Vine for the Centennial Celebration of the hundredth anniversary of the Negro Leagues. I had the opportunity to be present that day for the kick-off celebration of the Negro Leagues. The NLBM is the world's only museum dedicated to preserving the rich history of African-American baseball and its impact on the social advancement of America. The NLBM is a privately funded, 501c3 not-for-profit organization, incorporated in 1990. The NLBM operates two blocks from the Paseo YMCA where the Negro National League was founded by Andrew "Rube" Foster in 1920.[6]

On February 13, 1920, Andrew "Rube" Foster led eight independent black baseball team owners into a meeting held at the Paseo YMCA in Kansas City, Missouri. Out of that meeting came the birth of the Negro National League, the first successful, organized professional black baseball league that provided a playing field for African-American and Hispanic baseball players to showcase their world-class baseball skills and abilities. The Negro League would operate for forty years, becoming a catalyst for economic growth in African-American communities across the country, and would help spark social change in America.

100 Years Celebration

My first visit to the Negro Leagues Baseball Museum in Kansas City had been on June 8, 2002. My sons, VaShon and Torres, my father (their grandfather), Daniel Watkins, and I had a chance to visit, learn, and enjoy the rich history of Negro baseball players at the museum, the same rich history that is correlated in the NFL. Professional baseball and football here in the United States and worldwide are enjoyed by so many. The athleticism and speed that the athletes bring to their respective games of baseball and football is just incredible.

While visiting the museum in 2002, VaShon, my father, and I witnessed Torres run around the bases and touch home plate in the miniature baseball field in the museum. That was a thrill to see—a child having fun at four years of age. That was one of the proudest moments for his brother, my father, and me, to be present and watch that four-year-old having fun. The enjoyment I had with VaShon, Torres, and my father in 2002, inspired me to return to the Negro Leagues Baseball Museum for the 100th Anniversary Celebration of the Negro Leagues on February 13, 2020.

Just as my first high school teacher, Mr. Sherman Howard, was an African-American NFL pioneer, Mr. Andrew "Rube" Foster was a pioneer as well, albeit in baseball, and with my good fortune, I was able to be present for the Centennial Celebration of the NLBM. Mr. Foster, like Mr. George Stanley Halas, a participating founder of the NFL, was the founder of the Negro National League, the owner of the Chicago American Giants, and played on the Giants team as

My Look at the Chicago Bears
Professional Football Club

well as managed it. Mr. Foster and Mr. Halas, both players, each a founding father, albeit one in baseball and the other in football, were owners of their respective teams in Chicago. Mr. Foster helped to create, at that time in the year 1920, the largest black business in America. Mr. Halas had a hand, on September 17, 1920, in shaping what would later become the most lucrative sports league in the world. In the centennial year of the NFL, there were many people worldwide who cheered for their favorite NFL football players and teams. As the NFL celebrated its hundredth football season in 2019, it was the biggest sports organization in the world.

For Thursday Night Football, September 5, 2019, the hundredth NFL football season was rung in by the showcase game between the Chicago Bears versus the Green Bay Packers. The Thursday Night game in past years had been reserved for the previous season's Super Bowl champions. That season opener marked the 199th meeting of the two rivals, with the Green Bay Packers leading in victories 97 to 95, and six tie games.

That game on September 5, 2019, between the Bears and Packers, was the start of my nineteenth season working with the Chicago Bears chain crew in the NFL. The Green Bay Packers are said to be the most acclaimed franchise in NFL history. The Packers have won thirteen NFL Championships, the most all-time, and the Bears have won nine titles, second all-time, for the NFL record.

The Chicago Bears NFL Championships were won in the following seasons:

100 Years Celebration

- 1921 (the APFA Championship)[7]
- 1932
- 1933
- 1940
- 1941
- 1943
- 1946
- 1963
- 1985 (Super Bowl XX)

To my good fortune, the hundredth NFL football season was the first season I had the opportunity to work each of the Chicago Bears home games at historic Soldier Field. Starting with the Bears' season opener against the Green Bay Packers, the Bears home games in order during the course of the hundredth NFL season were played against the following:

- Minnesota Vikings
- New Orleans Saints
- Los Angeles Chargers
- Detroit Lions
- New York Giants
- Dallas Cowboys
- Kansas City Chiefs

This was an exciting and rewarding football season for me, especially to have the opportunity to work in the hundred years' existence of the Chicago Bears and the NFL. This was a unique football experience.

My Look at the Chicago Bears
Professional Football Club

The September 5, 2019 Thursday Night game was a fitting start to the hundredth NFL football season. The final score was:

           Green Bay Packers 10
           Chicago Bears   3

What a grand and splendid Thursday night in Chicago!

100 Years Celebration

**VaShon, Torres, and my father,
Daniel Watkins
June 8, 2002, Kansas City**

● ● ● ● ●

"The 2020 NFL football season is my twentieth season as a member of the officiating chain crew assigned to work the Chicago Bears home games at historic Soldier Field in Chicago."

Chapter 14

Overtime

In high school, college, and professional football in the NFL, an overtime period is a procedure that allows games with the score tied after the fourth quarter to be resolved, which means that there will be a winner of that contest. The teams are given more time to play so that a winner can be determined.

My Look at the Chicago Bears Football Club is going into overtime.

The Chicago Bears is one of the truly unique professional football teams in NFL history. May the Bears football team continue their unique success for the next hundred years, starting with the 2020 NFL football season.

The 2020 NFL football season is my twentieth season as a member of the officiating chain crew assigned to work the Chicago Bears home games at historic Soldier Field in Chicago.

My Look at the Chicago Bears Professional Football Club

I thank each of you for helping me along the way:

    Tony Alvizu

    Bryan Bulaga

    Mark Cheshareck

    Mark Endicott

    Wayne Endicott

    Joe Hall

    Tom Hall

    Laird Hayes

    George Hayward

    Marion Price

    Neal Pringle

    Ed Reier

    Joe Reier

    Mike Reier

    Calvin Saunders

    Harold Schwind

    Joe Slayton

    Gary Swanson

    Ken Trainor

Daniel Watkins

VaShon Watkins

Torres Williams

And I thank the countless others who are not mentioned by name in this writing. A heartfelt thank you to each of the football and basketball referees in Illinois and California where I have registered as a high school referee and worked both football and basketball games. My thanks also extend to the football and basketball referees I worked with as a collegiate referee.

It has been a joy and privilege to be a part of the Chicago Bears and the NFL, and I hope you have enjoyed reading what I have written.

Jerome Watkins

● ● ● ● ●

"This football game provided me with one of the proudest moments in my life, to look across this football field here at historic Soldier Field and see my son Torres working this NFL football game."

Chapter 15

Torres First Regular Season NFL Game

Sunday, January 3, 2021
Green Bay Packers vs. Chicago Bears

Torres had worked a previous NFL game, the Bears-Broncos pre-season game August 11, 2016 but this January 3rd, 2021, Torres had an opportunity to work the NFL's most played, most celebrated rivalry between the Green Bay Packers and Chicago Bears at historic Soldier Field. This game was the two hundred and two regular season game, with the Packers winning 100 games and the Bears winning 95 games, and 6 games ended in a tie score.

The final score today was Packers 35, Bears 16, The Packers one hundredth and first win against the Bears in this storied rivalry.

This last game of the regular NFL season has playoff implications. The Bears need to win to make the playoffs in one scenario and the Packers need to win this game to secure the number one seat in the National Football Conference. The Bears can also make the playoffs if the Arizona Cardinals lose their last regular season game today.

My Look at the Chicago Bears Professional Football Club

On this day, January 3, 2021 the Bears lost their game to the Packers, and the Cardinals lost their game against the Los Angeles Rams. The Bears were able to make the NFL playoffs with 8 wins and 8 losses this season.

The 2020 NFL season was a unique football season unlike any other season in the history of the NFL, the one hundredth and first NFL season, began like no other season.

Research and medical reports show that COVID 19 was first noticed in December, 2019 and arose out of Wuhan China. Unbeknownst to the wider world on January 24, 2020 is the date of the very first COVID 19 diagnosis, the first coronavirus case. The beginning of a worldwide pandemic.

The COVID 19 disease is a contagious disease caused by severe acute respiratory syndrome. The medical discovery of the coronavirus caused the year 2020 to be unlike any other year in millions and millions of peoples lives worldwide and the virus was also known as a global pandemic.

Torres and I had to take a coronavirus test before the Bears. Packers game this January 3, 2021. We both had a negative test result which allowed each of us to work this two hundred and second regular season game as father and son.

The coronavirus started to be more widely reported in February 2020 with several people being diagnosed with the virus in New York City, New York. As more and more adult age people were being diagnosed positively with this

Torres First Regular Season NFL Game

new virus at an alarming rate here in the United States and worldwide, the United States of America literally locked down in the middle of the month in March 2020.

This pandemic was causing people to test positive for the virus, and deaths began to mount as a result of people contracting the virus here in the United States and worldwide.

Due to the coronavirus, and to ensure safety precautions were followed, the NFL cancelled the entire 2020 pre-season, which means that there were no NFL pre-season games before the start of the one hundredth and first NFL football season.

The NFL allowed for each chain crew in the league to use only five chain crew members for each NFL game this season. The Chicago Bears would normally have eight chain crew members working the Bears home games. The 2020 season would now have only five chain crew members, which means one or two of the members would be responsible for two separate duties during each NFL game.

In the month of December 2020, one of the regular chain crew members had knee surgery, and two other members were physically injured, with one of the injured members being hospitalized. That meant that the chain crew would be short a person to work the Green Bay Packers vs. Chicago Bears game.

My son Torres had previously worked a pre-season game with the chain crew between the Chicago Bears and the

Denver Broncos August 11, 2016. Although there were three new members on the chain crew staff they had not had the opportunity to work a Bears home game to date.

The chain crew chief Harold Schwind asked Torres to work the Bears-Packers game on January 3, 2021. This would provide Torres an opportunity to work his second NFL game at historic Soldier Field, and his first regular season NFL game. Torres was being afforded an opportunity to work a game involving the oldest rivalry in the NFL during this 101st season.

Torres worked the position of Auxiliary Down Indicator, which means he would move down the field as the team advanced the ball or in the alternative lost yards, and have the indicator show the 1st, 2nd, 3rd or 4th down.

On this game day I worked the position of Down Indicator Operator for the 1st, 2nd, 3rd and 4th downs and my additional responsibility was to place the yardage clip for a possible measurement on each new 1st down. In working the position of Down Indicator Operator I wore the red vest which signifies that you are working that position which is the number one position on each chain crew for every NFL game.

Therefore, I was actually performing two duties on this game day, which was exciting for me, and I was very busy.

Torres First Regular Season
NFL Game

Torres and I practiced before the game, which in football language, was our pre-game preparation, where we went down the sideline of the football field. I was on the Packers sideline practicing and Torres was on the Bears sideline practicing. We were going to mirror each other during this game.

We took this father-son picture before the game.

Green Bay Packers vs. Chicago Bears January 3, 2021

My Look at the Chicago Bears
Professional Football Club

Torres was working the auxiliary down indicator on one teams sideline and I was working directly across the field on the other teams sideline. Torres and I would mirror each other during the entire game, and each one of us would show the same down on our respective indicators, even though I had the official indicator.

This game day is very significant and a highlight for me personally due to the fact that my first regular NFL game was between the Green Bay Packers and Chicago Bears on Veterans Day, Sunday, November 11, 2001. The football Head Linesman that was assigned to work the game was Mark Hittner.

Today, January 3, 2021, Torres first regular season NFL game between the Bears and Packers had NFL referee Mark Hittner assigned to work this game, the position of Down Judge. The NFL changed the name of Head Linesman to that of Down Judge. I was working on the same sideline with Mark and directly across the football field on the other teams sideline was Torres facing Mark and myself.

This football game provided me with one of the proudest moments in my life, to look across this football field here at historic Soldier Field and see my son Torres working this NFL football game.

Torres, when I am around you, life is the best and the best day is a day that I spend with you.

Torres First Regular Season
NFL Game

November 6, 2004
Oak Park, Illinois

From a ball boy at a High School football game on November 6, 2004 to the National Football League, the NFL, on January 3, 2021, the game between the Green Bay Packers vs. Chicago Bears at historic Soldier Field.

―――――――――――――| Notes |―――――――――――――

1. The city of Chicago became the first city in the nation to rename a city street for Dr. Martin Luther King, Jr.

2. On February 16, 1921, George Halas moved the franchise to Chicago where they played at what was called Cubs Park. Cubs Park was renamed Wrigley Field in 1926.

3. The NFL started their hundredth football season with 32 franchises, with the Chargers as the Los Angeles Chargers and the Rams as the Los Angeles Rams. The Raiders will start the 101st NFL football season as the Las Vegas Raiders.

4. As Mr. Jim Nantz, the CBS sportscaster, has so splendidly stated so many times, it is a feeling "unlike any other."

5. Dave Barrett is the musician and lyricist who composed and penned the lyrics to "One Shining Moment."

6. Negro Leagues Baseball Museum.

7. American Professional Football Association (APFA).

www.ingramcontent.com/pod-product-compliance
Lightning Source LLC
Chambersburg PA
CBHW042118100526
44587CB00025B/4106